FOREVER IN LOVE

ALSO BY JUNE COTNER

FOREVER IN LOVE

*A Celebration of Love
and Romance*

JUNE COTNER

**Andrews McMeel
Publishing, LLC**

Kansas City

06 07 08 09 10 FFG 10 9 8 7 6 5 4 3 2 1

ISBN-13: 978-0-7407-6156-0
ISBN-10: 0-7407-6156-0

Library of Congress Control Number: 2006923123

www.andrewsmcmeel.com

FOR JIM,
FOREVER.

CONTENTS

9   ☙ STRUGGLES ❧

14   ❦ REFLECTIONS ❦

A Letter to Readers

The selections in *Forever in Love* are a result of years collecting poems about love and marriage that touched me emotionally. When you say "I do," it is intended to be forever, and that's what we all want—a "forever" bond. Really, marriage is a perfect concept: Two individuals become partners, best friends, and allies for the rest of their days. While our society tends to idealize the lust-love of a new relationship, it's the true love of a long-term, committed relationship that is the ultimate dream for most of us. I hope this book will help couples realize that even during difficult times love creates bonds that will strengthen them in ways beyond what they could have only imagined when first married. Within these pages, you'll find an inspiring blueprint of the richness yet to come.

I have always been fascinated by the course of lifetime relationships between husbands and wives. The beginning of any relationship is filled with passion and grand dreams for the future. The early years bring a continued excitement and more thoughts about the reality of melding two lives—and perhaps a third with the arrival of a baby. By the time couples reach the middle years, they've encountered a number of struggles and challenges. The later years generally bring a mellowed acceptance of any differences, a greater appreciation for one's marriage, and an even deeper love for our life partners.

The last part of a relationship, the death of a spouse, is an inevitable part of life. I was deeply moved by the many excellent submissions I received for the "Partings" chapter. I found that these touching pieces gave me a greater appreciation for what I have today.

Forever in Love follows the path from "The Attraction" to "Mature Love" and many stages in between. It's a book that will allow couples to reminisce about earlier years together and look forward to the days to come.

My hope is that you will be moved, awed, and astonished by the kaleidoscope of feelings so eloquently expressed by the contributors in this book. The poets represented here have a fine gift for the interplay of words and emotions about the voyage through love and marriage. Even after many readings, some of the poems still bring tears to my eyes.

Thank you so much for picking up this book. Enjoy the journey—and each other!

THANKS

My sincere appreciation goes to my agent and friend, Denise Marcil. You are a tireless advocate for my books. I greatly value your unwavering support.

I send my heartfelt gratitude to Patty Rice, my talented and caring editor; and the backing of my enthusiastic publisher, Andrews McMeel Publishing.

I am deeply grateful to all the creative poets who have contributed to my books for over a decade now. I am constantly awed by the skill and insight reflected in your poems. Your words have truly blessed my life in countless ways.

For my loving husband, Jim Graves, thank you for providing the inspiration behind this book. I am fortunate to share life with you and love you more each day.

As always, thanks to my daughter, Kirsten Casey. I enjoy everything about you—and your help on the book has been priceless. I also appreciate the encouragement and support of my son, Kyle Myrvang; my sister, Susan Cotner; and my cousin, Margie Cotner Potts.

And most importantly, I thank God for blessing me with a life full of love as well as work that inspires me to be a better person.

ONE

THE SEARCH

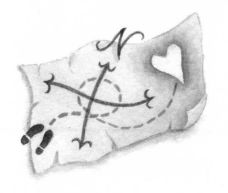

My Beautiful Love,
As Yet Unknown

My beautiful love as yet unknown
 you are living and breathing
 somewhere far away or perhaps quite close to me,
but I still know nothing
 of the threads that form the fabric of your life
 or the pattern which makes your face distinctive.

MICHEL QUOIST
(FRANCE, TWENTIETH CENTURY)

*The
Search*
❧ 2 ❧

IN TRANSIT

He comes to me
in dreams at night.
His eyes look through me
as his hands caress my face.
His words are as kind
as his laughter is playful.
I love the thief of my heart
and know him not
by daybreak.

JOAN NOËLDECHEN

THE BLUES

From across this quiet café,
your eyes tell me
I should abandon this poem,

should leave these words,
rise from this table
and come to your side.

Another might look the other way,
obey the Muse
and keep the poem going.

But it's the blue of your eyes that I'm after,
and the blues should never be played
alone.

CHARLES GHIGNA

*The
Search*

You, I Hope to Find

Though I don't know who you are yet
I can still imagine the strength and warmth of
your arms.
While your face isn't clear,
needing to find you is.
I know you're out there,
I just don't know where.
While we haven't found each other yet,
know I think of you every day.
I hope that you do the same.

LEAH KATHRYN SELL, AGE FIFTEEN

MY FIRST LOVE STORY

The minute I heard my first love story
I started looking for you, not knowing
how blind that was.

Lovers don't finally meet somewhere.
They're in each other all along.

RUMI
(1207– 1273)
TRANSLATED BY COLEMAN BARKS

THE ATTRACTION

HIM

I'm talking to my friends at my locker,
not paying attention to much of anything.
Then, I get up and turn around
Behind me, *he* is standing.
His smile melts me.
"Hi," I finally manage to say.
He waves, then walks away.
Slowly, all feeling comes back to me.
Hi? I think to myself,
angered that I hadn't said more . . .
hadn't kept him longer.
Later in class,
I can't help but steal a glance at him;
He's looking at me too!
I quickly turn back to my paper.
Now I lay in bed,
wishing I knew how he felt about me—
wishing I knew how *I* looked in *his* eyes.
I close my ears to all sound, my eyes to all sight.

The
Attraction
❧ *8* ❧

In my mind, I see him smiling, his brown eyes
  glowing.
I make up my mind:
Tomorrow I will tell him how I feel.

JENNIFER LYNN CLAY, AGE TWELVE

The
Attraction
❦ 9 ❦

Transforming Love

When John Denver wrote "Annie's Song"
I wanted to be Annie.
Then I just wanted someone
to write a love song
and sing it to me
for all the world to hear.
I wanted to be loved.

But since I met you,
I want to be me.
I want to be the poet,
the singer,
the lover.

JEAN ROACH

BROWN EYES

When you smiled,
the edges of your cheeks
dissolving
into a thousand wrinkles
and your wide brown eyes
reflecting the sun,
I wanted to hug you
there in the square
before the whole world
as if no one,
no thing but you
ever existed.

SUSAN LANDON

SEEING YOU

Seeing you
without warning

after staying away
so long

the heart I thought
I'd subdued

tore loose
and ran straight

into April's
green dazzle

into the light
of your hazel eyes

leaving the rest
of me numb.

Stunned
with love.

MARJORIE ROMMEL

The
Attraction

I Think I Am in Love

When I see you I feel wonderful
My heart beats like a drum
I walk on white, fluffy clouds
I think I am in love.

The butterflies inside me come alive
My tongue ties in a knot
I float in the clear, blue sky
I think I am in love.

I'm on top of the world
I become so alive
I do everything just so you'll notice me
I think I am in love.

All these feelings are gold to me
Even if you are just a crush
Some people think I'm "too young" for this
But I still think I am in love.

CASSIE HIDDLESON, AGE THIRTEEN

The
Attraction
❧ 13 ❧

THREE

LONGING

SAY

If you say you love me—even once
I will run into your arms
Swifter than the mad March wind
Or the trembling doe in the palm-fringed woods
I will adore you, worship you
Like the God of the sun-up hour
Say, my own, say you love me.

MOUSHUMI CHAKRABARTY

WILD NIGHTS! WILD NIGHTS!

Wild Nights—Wild Nights!
Were I with thee
Wild Nights should be
Our luxury!

Futile—the Winds—
To a Heart in port—
Done with the Compass—
Done with the Chart!

Rowing in Eden—
Ah, the Sea!
Might I but moor—Tonight—
In Thee!

EMILY DICKINSON
(1830–1886)

While I Asked Myself

While I asked myself
Whether you might be coming
Or I might go there,
The hesitant moon appeared,
And I slept, the door unlocked.

AUTHOR UNKNOWN

At the Half-Chance of Being Loved

I perfume my body with oils,
I put jasmine in my hair.
Ashamed of my new priority
I used to be smarter than this.

Gathering sticks for my fire,
washing my linens at the river stone,
my chores glimmer with new radiance
at the half-chance of being loved.

I would weave a cloth shirt for your shoulders,
that I could always be touching your skin.
This village seemed so plain before,
now everything in it glows.

INGRID GOFF-MAIDOFF

My Heart

My heart is pouring itself out to me.
My heart is soaring toward you over thousands
  of miles.
My heart comes nearer and nearer.
My heart longs to enter.

Like ten fingers running over the keys,
like a powerful stream that has ever been flowing,
like a flock of night birds lit by the moon—
I am flying after my heart.

JANINE CANAN

APPOGGIATURA

Lover, beloved, hoped-for one, listen:

Away from you, I'm as pale as the moon by day, a
   winter afternoon.

Antlers glisten in the dying light—deer draw near. I
   curl up like a snail,

or like drying leaves, lying on the riverbank, my ear
   to the earth, eavesdropping.

Rock's heart beats, gravity sighs, my breath knocks
   against cold clay; I hear death

keeping time until at last the land lies mute. There's
   sand in my eyes, salt in my tears.

I make shale my pillow, sleeping, having hanged my
   harp upon the willow, weeping.

KELLY CHERRY

ONLY YOU

No being in all the wide realms of heaven
or across this vast earth
can understand my desperate longing.
Only You.
Only You.

RAMPRASAD SEN
(1718– 1775)

F O U R

⁓

COURTSHIP

The Bait

Come live with me, and be my love,
And we will some new pleasures prove
Of golden sands, and crystal brooks,
With silken lines, and silver hooks.

JOHN DONNE
(1572–1631)

EVERY KISS PROVOKES ANOTHER

Every kiss provokes another. Ah, in those earliest
days of love how naturally the kisses spring into life.
How closely, in their abundance, are they pressed one
against another; until lovers would find it as hard to
count the kisses exchanged in an hour, as to count
the flowers in a meadow in May.

MARCEL PROUST
(1871–1922)

QUESTIONS

I would like to lean with you on a dune
overlooking the voluptuous sea, and ask
what wind called you to this place?
Was it hunger, or a song?
What are the worlds you left behind?
Have you ever known a paradise?
Could you tell it to me now?
What pleasures do you count living here?
What foods are most delicious,
what aromas most divine?
How do you prefer the shape of the moon?
Do the seasons hold equal beauty,
is there one you favor more?
Who did you trust
riding through your tender years?
Do you envy the bliss of others,
or long for it,
equal to your own?

Courtship

What do you court, worship,
gather to hold dear?
In my mind I'd like to kiss you,
but I'd ask these questions first.

INGRID GOFF-MAIDOFF

Courtship

Last Name

I hate to admit it, but I have thought about how my
   name will sound if I take your last name.

I have even practiced the signature (I know, shame!
   shame!).

I will not scare you by telling you this. I will just
   keep the name humming through my hot little
   head like a mantra until it is time.

I can't wait for that time to come!

KIRSTEN CASEY

MERGING

THE KISS

Kiss me.
Take me to the peaceful shore and lay me down
that I may be strong.
Your love caresses my body
and our two souls become one.
Kiss me.
We fall into each other by the rhythm
of our breathing.
My heart is open, come inside.
Kiss me.

      Kiss me.

            Kiss me.

LORI EBERHARDY

Merging

REMEMBERING

Come here, closer, and fold
into the dent of my chest,
the crook of my shoulder.
In the open window the
candle betrays the wind's
summer breath and the
night settles down around us.

Don't move, not now,
let's be still, hold this moment
before we open our bodies,
and tell me, one more time,
how you came to find me.

STEPHEN J. LYONS

Merging
❦ *31* ❦

A Love Song

Out of golden breath
heaven created us.
O how we love one another.

Birds become buds on the branches
and roses flutter away.

I search for your lips
behind a thousand kisses.

Night made from gold,
stars made from night—
no one can see us.

When day brings the green,
we'll be slumbering—
our shoulders playing like butterflies.

ELSE LASKER-SCHÜLER
(1869–1945)
TRANSLATED BY JANINE CANAN

Merging
❧ 32 ☙

NOW!

Out of your whole life give but a moment!
      All of your life that has gone before,
      All to come after it,—so you ignore,
So you make perfect the present; condense,
In a rapture of rage, for perfection's endowment,
Thought and feeling and soul and sense,
Merged in a moment which give me at last
You around me for once, you beneath me, above me—
Me, sure that, despite of time future, time past,
This tick of lifetime's one moment you love me!
How long such suspension may linger? Ah, Sweet,
      The moment eternal—just that and no more—
      When ecstasy's utmost we clutch at the core,
While cheeks burn, arms open, eyes shut and lips
  meet!

ROBERT BROWNING
(1812–1889)

Merging
❧ *33* ❧

BELOVED

My soul quietly flows into you
and as you lead me to your gentle embrace,
I exhale and welcome the peace that is
the perfect promise of you.

As your arms hold me safe I realize
my love for you is strong,
my belief in you is limitless,
my admiration for you is constant.

All my wishes have been granted,
and I cherish these quiet blessings you have
given me on this side of heaven.

LORI EBERHARDY

Merging
❧ 34 ❧

REQUEST

If you say
you love me more
than the light
of each and
every star,
it is not
enough.
I want
the lonesome—
beauty-evening
of Earth
included too.

VIRGINIA BARRETT

COMMITMENT

This Night

This night there are
no limits
to what may be given.

This is not a night but
a marriage,
a couple whispering in bed in
unison
the same words.

Darkness simply lets down a
curtain for that.

RUMI
(1207–1273)
TRANSLATED BY COLEMAN BARKS

Night Secret

I have chosen you
among all these stars.

Am awake, a listening flower
in the humming bush.

Our lips long to make honey,
our shimmering nights in full bloom.

From your body's holy spark
my heart lights its heavens.

All my dreams hang from your gold.
I have chosen you among all these stars.

ELSE LASKER-SCHÜLER
(1869–1945)
TRANSLATED BY JANINE CANAN

BASKET OF FIGS

Bring me your pain, love. Spread
it out like fine rugs, silk sashes,
warm eggs, cinnamon
and cloves in burlap sacks. Show me

the detail, the intricate embroidery
on the collar, tiny shell buttons,
the hem stitched the way you were taught,
pricking just a thread, almost invisible.

Unclasp it like jewels, the gold
still hot from your body. Empty
your basket of figs. Spill your wine.

That hard nugget of pain, I would suck it,
cradling it on my tongue like the slick
seed of pomegranate. I would lift it

tenderly, as a great animal might
carry a small one in the private
cave of the mouth.

Commitment
❦ *40* ❦

ELLEN BASS

A HEART FULL OF LOVE

Sometimes it is invisible and at times it is silent.
But in the still of the night,
it speaks to my heart and sings to my soul.

Your love has turned little pieces of nothing into
  a dream
because you said four simple words,
"I believe in you."
A promise strengthened by encouragement becomes
  a gift.
My spirit is strong and my faith is restored.
You have become my dream.

It is carried in the whisper of the breeze,
and it is when I need it the most
that I feel it the strongest.

Your love stirs and grows in my heart.
My hesitance gives way to your conviction and
  I find my way
closer to your center, ultimately my salvation.
Your love has saved my love.

LORI EBERHARDY

UNCONDITIONAL

The day proceeds in silent motion,
light waves lapping against
the evening,
distant shore where I,
a swimmer of solitude,
wait to climb into your arms
once more.

And it is not your smile
that warms me
nor your kiss
but the simple sight of your face,
the one who loves me in triumph and disgrace,
just this . . .

ARLENE GAY LEVINE

Although I Conquer All the Earth

Although I conquer all the earth,

Yet for me there is only one city.

In that city there is for me only one house;

And in that house, one room only;

And in that room, a bed.

And one woman sleeps there,

The shining joy and jewel of all my kingdom.

AUTHOR UNKNOWN
(ANCIENT INDIA)

DOUBLE IMAGE

Hours after the ceremony, my husband
keeps admiring his new wedding ring.
He invites me to examine his band,
although I wear an identical one, smaller.

Look, you can see our faces in the gold,
he shows me. Our tiny reflection
reminds me of van Eyck's wedding portrait,[1]
the miniature images of a bride and groom
mirrored in a convex glass behind them.

Now when we're apart, I envision my husband
holding this impression of me close,
pressed tenderly within his hand.

MARY KOLADA SCOTT

1. *The Arnolfini Marriage*

GIVE ME TEN MORE YEARS

And I still could not tell you
any more than right now about
how brown your eyes are to me,
about how your voice is always
the best first sound I hear
each morning, about how even
your fragrance in an empty room
lifts me up and sends me searching,
about how your long legs in summer shorts
make me want to run outside
and jump so high I might just
catch hold of a cloud, might just
find you already there smiling
with your arms outstretched
letting me know this is where we are,
this is where we will always be.

CHARLES GHIGNA

THE GIFT

In the lines of your face: sacred space.
Your eyes, pristine—a place to float
peacefully in otherwise turbulent waters.
How lucky I am to have
your honest heart for an anchor.
How grateful I am for the smile
that melts icebergs in a sea
of frail humanity.
How blessed it is in this desperate,
beautiful world to know and hold
the reason for being here, my love,
happening upon your light
and remembering,
this is the gift.

ARLENE GAY LEVINE

Commitment
❧ 46 ❧

OATH OF FRIENDSHIP

Shang ya!
I want to be your friend
For ever and ever without break or decay.
When the hills are all flat
And the rivers are all dry,
When it lightnings and thunders in winter,
When it rains and snows in summer,
When Heaven and Earth mingle—
Not till then will I part from you.

AUTHOR UNKNOWN
(CHINA, FIRST CENTURY BC)

EARLY YEARS

First House

On the edge of town,
a world in building.
Acres of houses,
one of them ours.

We get out and survey
in sunlight—I the future
garden, veggies and flowers,
you the roof and gutters.
We cannot look enough.

Inside, the rooms only roughed in.
So much space to fill!
The sofa here. No, there.
We can hardly wait.

Hand in hand we walk back
to the car. A butterfly
is resting on a bulldozer.
I shall have yellow curtains

in the kitchen, to flutter in
the breeze at the open window—
yellow bright and sheer as those wings.

IDA FASEL

LOVE POEM

She prefers a quiet walk along the shore.
Mozart. Dry white wine.
Movies with a melancholic touch.

His spirit soars with beer.
A John Wayne flick.
The rumble of his motorcycle.

Yet,
When he holds her,
When he takes her in . . .

Stars swoon.
Rivers bend.
Mountains cease their heaving.

Unborn babes
long to hear their names.

JO-ANNE ROWLEY

ROOTS

Daily, my heart grows roots
in this ground where we live,

roots arcing down
like hands
embracing soil,

meeting underground rivers
and moving through rock
on their way to the molten
core,

the circle
where the fire begins.

ANDREA POTOS

Marriage Takes Work

All those "and they lived happily ever after" fairy-tale endings need to be changed to "and they began the very hard work of making their marriages happy."

LINDA MILES

SUMMER ON THE FARM

This is our evening ritual,
after supper, before bed,
to put a chenille throw rug
and a feather pillow
in the rusty Radio Flier,
lay our toddler snugly,
and walk west on the blacktop
toward maturing corn
that waves its tassels
in a strip of red-orange sky,
just walk without interrupting
the crickets or the baby's babbling
or, flashing their tiny torches
just above the bean field,
the fireflies, soon to join
their homebound cousins
the fixed stars
in the night sky.

MAUREEN TOLMAN FLANNERY

WE CAN

The challenge is to . . . turn "I Do" into "We Can."

SCOTT STANLEY

DAILY LIFE

ORDINARY LIFE

This was a day when nothing happened,
the children went off to school
without a murmur, remembering
their books, lunches, gloves.
All morning, the baby and I built block stacks
in the squares of light on the floor.
And lunch blended into naptime,
I cleaned out kitchen cupboards,
one of those jobs that never gets done,
then sat in a circle of sunlight
and drank ginger tea,
watched the birds at the feeder
jostle over lunch's little scraps.
A pheasant strutted from the hedgerow,
preened and flashed his jeweled head.
Now a chicken roasts in the pan,
and the children return,
the murmur of their stories dappling the air.
I peel carrots and potatoes without paring my
thumb.

We listen together for your wheels on the drive.
Grace before bread.
And at the table, actual conversation,
no bickering or pokes.
And then, the drift into homework.
The baby goes to his cars, drives them
along the sofa's ridges and hills.
Leaning by the counter, we steal a long slow kiss,
tasting of coffee and cream.
The chicken's diminished to skin and skeleton,
the moon to a comma, a sliver of white,
but this has been a day of grace
in the dead of winter,
the hard cold knuckle of the year,
a day that unwrapped itself
like an unexpected gift,
and the stars turn on,
order themselves
into the winter night.

BARBARA CROOKER

WARRANTY

Side by side we perform a
routine, tedious task.
Updating the warranty file,
discarding the old,
inserting the new.
Not very sexy, and yet . . .

Sifting through slips of paper,
day-to-day unspoken promises
to be there, whatever,
regardless, despite,
for two years, ten years,
twenty years more,
till we wear out and expire.

For sheer romance,
soft music and candlelight
can't touch it.

ANN REISFELD BOUTTÉ

Away in Virginia, I See a Mustard Field and Think of You

because the blue hills are like the shoulders and slopes
of your back as you sleep. Often, I slip a hand under
your body to anchor myself to this earth. The yellow
mustard rises from a waving sea of green.

I think of us driving narrow roads in France, under
a tunnel of sycamores, my hair blowing in the hot
  wind,
opera washing out of the radio, loud. We are feeding
each other cherries from a white paper sack.

And then we return to everyday life, where we fall
into bed exhausted, fall asleep while still reading,
forget the solid planes of the body in the country
of dreams. I miss your underwear, soft from a
thousand washings, the socks you still wear from a
store out of business thirty years. I love to smell your
sweat after mowing grass or hauling wood; I miss the
weight on your side of the bed.

BARBARA CROOKER

FROM THE ASTRONAUT OF YOUR HEART

Every time you leave our Earth,
I sit in the empty launching pad of our home
and wait for your return.

I fill your chair at the table
with what is left of my weightless self.
I sleep on your side of the bed,
drive your car instead of mine,
wash and fold your laundry as though
you are already here to wear it.

I stare at the TV as though it were your face,
say good morning to the radio
as though it held your ears.
I dress for work and talk to it
of where we've been, of where you are,
of when you're coming home.

I am no John Glenn,
no Shepard, no Armstrong.

I am not even me when you are gone.
I am only a lonely astronaut
lost inside your space.

CHARLES GHIGNA

Daily
Life
❧ *63* ❧

LOVE LIFE

Love,
You are not all
I dreamed of,
You are way too serious
Way too quiet—
So difficult to reach,
Sometimes

But then,
I'm not everything you wished for
I'm sure,
I seek conversation
Make short stories long,
When facts will do—
I know

Yet here we are,
I love your calmness
Even in the harsh moments
You love

My details in the rush
I admire your push,
You appreciate
my type of beauty

We are living the life we chose
And loving it.

ZORAIDA RIVERA MORALES

To Turn from My Forgetting

So often we have fallen,
too weary for love,
into that rich, secret realm
between living and dying
which we nightly traverse,
and as often next morning returned,
faces blank,
our memory pockets pulled inside out,
having lost our souvenirs . . .

What astonishes me, always,
is to turn from my forgetting
and to recall
that there are whole villages inside you, Love
where I have yet to travel.
Each has its own pub, town character,
and bawdy national song.
There are mountainous landscapes,
forests thick with foliage and vine,
rivers rushing by, studded with stepping stones.
There are moss banks, inviting rest.
Did they come in through your eyes,
your ears, your full sensuous mouth?

Or did they, on some interior parallel, grow
like you, from seed?

I am remembering your kisses last night,
how the streetlight spilled onto the bed,
a stowaway,
how the children breathed even sleeping breaths
in the next room.
Now my heart holds a slow, radiant fire
as I tend to the day's details
(each a kind of grace)
our clothes to wash, children to chauffeur,
carrots and potatoes to peel and stew,
floors to sweep,
bread, fruit, honey to buy at the market . . .

And you stand heightened handsome
as you don your derby hat.
I glimpse echoes of your grandfathers,
old yellowing photographs, in black and white . . .
We too will die someday, you and I.
I am, for a moment, unafraid of that continuum.
(I eat it like a peach.)

INGRID GOFF-MAIDOFF

Upon Awakening

You cup my hand
against your cheek
on the pillow;
you tilt your head
and kiss my wrist,
whisking away
all the worries
of today.

DONNA WAHLERT

WHY

for your great bear of a body
for not making fun of my hats
for your gifts of presence and possibility
for being as sweet as honey thick in the jar
for opening up new states of being to me
for being such a pain in the ass
for your loudest shout of joy, your smallest twinkle
for washing the dishes
for the way my body sings at your touch, your voice
for accepting my need for light and ocean
for making me bread for body and soul
for getting out of the way when my buttons
  get pushed
for bringing me my unheard voice
for allowing yourself to open to the inundation
  of my love
for knowing that we both need intermittent solitude
for your wonder at my logic and our spiraling
  conversations
for your deepest pain and tears
for you, whole and holy
for you

NITA PENFOLD

SMALL FAILURES AS A WIFE

I never greeted my husband at the door, like our
  dog did, all excited and breathless.
I never read *Men Are from Mars, Women Are from Venus*.
I never knew where I put the emergency flashlight,
and when I did find it,
  the batteries were always dead.
I never made beds with a hospital corner.
I never recalled where I hid our birth certificates or
  auto pink slips.
I never could relate to or strive to be like Martha
  Stewart.
I never ironed my husband's pants with the crease
  in the same place.
I never could bring myself to clean grout with a
  toothbrush.
I never found out where our dog, Sparky, buried
  my mother-in-law's hearing aid.
I never potted a plant that didn't die.
I never forgave my husband for missing Back to
  School Night in '95.

I never cleaned a bathroom without feeling like
   poor Cinderella.
I never remembered to cancel the newspaper when
   we went on vacation.

Now that I think about it, I never appreciated what
   an understanding man
         my husband really is!

SUSAN R. NORTON

HUSBAND OUT OF TOWN
THINKS ABOUT HIS WIFE

He hopes she is
sitting in the sunlight,
listening to Bach.
He knows how much
she likes it in their house,
her house, all by herself.

What he doesn't know is:
she and the house in late afternoon
long like the cottonwood leaves
and banks of the river
for the last lingering sun fingers.
For him. For him.

BARBARA SCHMITZ

FINDING US IN JACKSON POLLACK

Within the spiral splashes,
dots and dashes, dribble-color-canvas—
splattered scenes through which we walk
and run our days away, all directions
taking us the thousand ways in which
it seems we never can connect,
sometimes, despite the odds
you and I,
careening carelessly, bump in an instant-
time, and like a cluster-clump of paint,
though small in his wild art, we intersect.

PEARL STEIN SELINSKY

Daily
Life
❧ *73* ❧

THE BEST PART

First we fall in love. That's the exciting part. Then we learn to love. That's the hard part. Finally, we simply love being loving. And that, by far, is the best part.

MICHAEL LEACH

CHOICES

The Mall shuts out the world—
what the sky is up to, heft of wind.
We have our choice of popcorn
and four theaters. Giant forms

crowd the screen's edge, heads
cropped. Mouths open wide
and thunder like ocean-swept caves.
The music is earsplitting.
But under the little boom box
projecting a ray of light,
dusty, restless, filled with
shoot-outs, smashed-ups, flames,

our hands seek each other out,
two little birds nestling close,
not making a sound
but bursting with song.

IDA FASEL

Daily
Life
❦ 75 ❦

GRATITUDE

I woke early to the sound
of the first autumn storm
rattle the windows
like small river stones. I felt
my wife's body curled warm
around the circles of our two cats,
and through the adjoining wall
I could hear my daughter's
steady breathing and picture
her asleep under sheets and quilts.

I lay there in the dark wanting
nothing else. I could imagine
no other life, past or future,
only this one listening
to rain wash away summer's dust
down the hill
past all the other homes
to the highway where it was
still quiet. No trucks. No cars.
No one going anywhere.

STEPHEN J. LYONS

IN THIS SEASON

The sun
slips out early.
Trees release
their long blue shadows
in the snow,
and dream of leaves
and feathers.

Everything softens
in this hour,
the light outside the windows
and the light behind our eyes.
We lay the fire
and find our ways
to keep each other warm.

DEBORAH GORDON COOPER

In the Middle

of a life that's as complicated as everyone else's,
struggling for balance, juggling time.
The mantle clock that was my grandfather's
has stopped at 9:20; we haven't had time
to get it repaired. The brass pendulum is still,
the chimes don't ring. One day you look out the
  window,
green summer, the next, and the leaves have already
  fallen,
and a gray sky lowers the horizon. Our children
  almost grown,
our parents gone, it happened so fast. Each day, we
  must learn again how to love, between morning's
  quick coffee
and evening's slow return. Steam from a pot of
  soup rises,
mixing with the yeasty smell of baking bread.
Our bodies twine, and the big black dog pushes his
great head between;

his tail is a metronome, three-quarter time. We'll
   never get there,
Time is always ahead of us, running down the
   beach, urging us on faster, faster, but sometimes
   we take off our watches, sometimes we lie in the
   hammock, caught between the mesh of rope and
   the net of stars, suspended, tangled up in love,
   running out of time.

BARBARA CROOKER

STRUGGLES

Marriage Work

"You have to work at a marriage,"
they told me
when I was twenty,
and storybook naive.

I felt sorry for them then,
thinking all those prophets
had simply picked
the wrong mate.

But that was before
I stopped
reading fairy tales,
before I gave up
childhood dreams,

Before I was twenty years married,
and first began
the hard work of
a marriage.

ELAYNE CLIFT

SURVIVING THE SEASONS

> If you look at marriage as long term . . . there are
> good and bad seasons. . . . Maybe even some years
> you have to struggle through. It's like . . . farming.
> You don't leave the land after a bad harvest or two.

FRAN KUPFER

ANOTHER NEW ENGLAND WINTER

By February we're weary.
Four o'clock's darkness
descends again over
our sterile snow drifts,
trapping us behind doors,
drawn curtains that keep
drafts and neighbors at bay.
Even diehard Yankees wonder
if spring will come.

We've faced such dormancy
before: five years waiting
for a tiny life to flower
inside my womb. Then, too,
we shut shades early
against sounds, voices
of nearby children
sledding into our gully,
alone with Mourning.

Come March, we notice
first buds unfurling.
We crack our windows;
let light breezes in,
carrying pollen, fresh and sticky,
to our sills. We savor
this vibrant yellow-green
reminder of season's change
enough to say, *We're survivors,*
lovers of spring.

NANCY TUPPER LING

COOPERATION

Marriage is that intimate relationship which tugs and pulls at two egos in order to create the fulfillment of each other—if only we can humble ourselves enough to cooperate.

HENRY JAMES BOYRS

How to Return to Your Husband

Find a spot that is sunny.
Let the breeze touch your face.
Stop running. Let your heart
stay in one place. Look
at what you have together
already done. It is not over.
You are both new now,
and you have come a long way.
But continue. Have faith
in what has already begun.

CASSIE PREMO STEELE

Struggles

LONG AFTER THE LOSS

They made an unspoken pact between them
to bury grief somewhere in the house
where the throaty sound of laughter still jumped out
from behind a doorway at unexpected times
to grab the ankles of their recovery.

The pain itself was hard in the center,
but sticky to the touch and gray-fuzzed on the surface
like a piece of fruit long forgotten in the bottom
of a bag of important papers.

Sometimes she would find it
under a clean stack of folded towels
or, reaching for the right spice, she might
touch it in the back of a pantry cupboard.

It caught him off guard in a tool chest
near the tack hammer half the size of the one
  he used.

Mostly they just stuck the grief
back into another place
and went on their way of a hobbled day
as if running a three-legged race
in which they kept falling down together.
But sometimes one of them would take it up
and try to know it better,
like a curious derelict old acquaintance
or hold onto it tightly
through the spores and mold-dust
and try to toss it out of the house.

MAUREEN TOLMAN FLANNERY

CALLING TRUCE

How about this: I promise to stop bringing up your family and how you remind me so much of your father—if you promise to stop saying that all I ever do is complain and that nothing is ever good enough for me.

For right now, can we just be quiet? Stop yelling. Can we sit on the couch and take some long, slow breaths? Honestly, I love you so much but it is just hard for me to feel it right now. How about that Christmas Eve when we stayed up all night laughing, talking, and joking around? See, we do have fun; we just haven't had much lately. Let's be buddies again. I am calling truce.

KARI LANE

Sleeping with You

Is there anything more wonderful?
After we have floundered
through our separate pain

we come to this, I bind myself to you,
like otters wrap in kelp, so the current
will not steal us as we sleep.

Through the night we turn together,
rocked in the shallow surf,
pebbles polished by the sea.

ELLEN BASS

MATURE LOVE

TENTH ANNIVERSARY

Ten years ago, after the first night
we spent together,
we went to pick strawberries
knee-deep in furrows of scalloped leaves,
white flowers winking like stars.
It's still early morning
but we're drunk on the winy air
and the headiness of our desire.
As we kissed more than we picked,
our mouths brushed like petals
rubbing in the wind,
our crimson fingers strayed
beyond boundaries of clothing.
Stitch us in that tapestry forever,
baskets full of berries, and always in love . . .
But we had to go home,
turn the fresh fruit into preserves:
hull and cull the berries, crush them
with lemon, boil until thick
and sweet with yearning and sun.
Sealed in wax, each jar's stained glass,

full of the light.
And when we spread this redness
on morning toast, sparks
rekindle and glow.

And now it's ten years later.
Strawberry picking's an annual
task I do alone, or with a friend.
I boil the jam down to the clatter
of children underfoot.
And our eyes meet over curly heads
and our hands brush like green leaves in the wind . . .
And the jam shines in its cathedral of wax,
the sweetness of early June
poured in glass jars.
On January mornings,
when love and light are memories,
these red suns
light our cellar shelf.

BARBARA CROOKER

IN THE LIGHT OF ANOTHER MOON

I look at you and cannot stop
the passion that surges to life,
my heart yearning as it did
     the very first time,
and I want to do with you
what autumn does to maple leaves
and northern light to sky

MARIAN OLSON

FOR MY BELOVED

I have, in a moment,
fallen in love with you again.
I don't know what it was—
a touch, the smooth stroke of skin on skin, a look
    of tender delight . . .
I don't know what it was that unlocked the door,
but there it was—again.
Not the deep love that is always there,
even when layered over with the everydayness
    of living.
No. Beloved,
ever my Beloved,
in that moment
what awoke from slumber was the in-love-ness
    of love,
bright, fresh, and alive;
the wonder of you,
the joy in us.

DAWN B. MUNDY

To My Husband on Our Anniversary

No longer
Do I crave the latest styles,
Nor does a front-row seat mean
All that it used to.

And if it should happen
That our house burns down,
And with it, my books,
No doubt
I would still go on.

But for you, love,
Swift shadow to my soul,
I am still a monument
Of desire.

MARYANNE HANNAN

Mature
Love
❧ 98 ❧

THEIR ADVENTURES

I never thought we'd live through them.
We were the generation that could do it all—
stop a war and discover a world,
Europe on $5 a Day, street eating
across Mexico, lure of the different
and the far away, follow the Dead
or the Doors, join the Peace Corps,
"Live and Work Abroad,"
that brochure sat in a drawer
while I conceived four reasons
why not to go this year,
and here we are,
they with the backpacks
boarding the flight,
we on the ground feeling
strangely disoriented.
Perhaps we had to think it first,
for their adventures sprouted in our dreams.

MAUREEN TOLMAN FLANNERY

*Mature
Love*
❧ 99 ❧

First Kiss

Do you remember
our first kiss
as we stood nervously
under cozy-warm porch light?

The night was hushed and quiet
except for the sound of our
young hearts beating.

You leaned down toward me.
A breeze wrapped around us
like a caress. Your gentle lips
persuaded mine, soft
and sweet as cotton candy.
We savored sensation
tasted each other slowly.
Mouths spoke without words.
Eyes closed, yet
we saw deeply into
each other's self and essence.

Unspoken promises filled us
with dreams of our tomorrows
that we remember today.

SHERRI WAAS SHUNFENTHAL

ANNIVERSARY

She sits on the beach
and watches honeyed couples
cling across the sand.

Her hair like silvered sea oats now,
she gazes at the sun
spins visions of her old loves.

The first flew off like Icarus
and lived above the clouds
piloting jet planes.

The next melted
into liquid columns of figures
in his accounting ledger.

The engineer built himself a
bridge to Canada when she told him
she couldn't see them together on the horizon.

Mature
Love
❧ 102 ❧

The last ran over her heart
with his Volkswagen Beetle
and his singular shyness.

She turns to him now
on their shell-anchored blanket;
he pats her sandy knee.
Thirty years of waves have washed
his shyness into quiet fidelity.

DONNA WAHLERT

MY WIFE BREAKS OUT

This afternoon she flashed me,
she who's always been so shy,
perfect circles of softness
staring at my face, then gone,
hidden beneath her sweater.

I just smiled.
It was the middle of the day,
her flash an interruption,
a suggestion she's leaving her room,
full-force, unchained,
ready to take the world by surprise.

BOB SLAYMAKER

AFTER ALL THESE YEARS OF LOVING YOU

I feel almost afraid that I have used
up my quota of happiness, that
you'll soon be disappearing
like champagne bubbles,
popping in the air,
leaving behind
a tiny mist
of regret
to prove
to me
that
you
were
ever
here
at all.

SUSAN R. NORTON

POSSIBLY

When I left Pennsylvania, spring was still
scuffing her feet, scarf muffled around her neck,
duffel coat buttoned up tight, the ground still
hard as a calculus textbook, grass infinite shades
of dun and tan, the scruffy pelt of something dead
by the road, trees and branches bare.
I was heavy as lead, the low gray sky, cold front
moving in, calendar flipping back to March.
You and I sat in separate rooms with our separate
books, at odds and elbows; our busy lives
with their datebooks and daytimers filling in
the blanks. But I'm coming back now,
sweet as birdsong, right as rain, new poems
in my notebook that flutter from my elbows
and wrists like those first new leaves
that suddenly appear on a warm day.
And now it is the hour of lemon light, forsythia
wands shooting sparks over the new grass,
daffodils showering gold in the wind.

It is the season of possibility, when anything
might happen. Two stubborn people, dulled
into habit, stuck in the old sock of marriage,
might just fall in love again, watch the sun set
behind the orchard, watch the sky turn lilac
and lavender, feel the spring stars click
into their new stories, soft air on their arms,
soft breath in the mouth. They might start
to do the old dance, the spring dance, the clothes
are in the way dance, the return of blue scilla
skies dance, the rub lilac blossoms all over
your skin dance, they might let the evening come.

BARBARA CROOKER

*Mature
Love*

MAGIC

For twenty-five years we
have been living together. Are
we now an old married couple?
This morning we woke up
with the same old song
going through each of our heads.
The song was the old, old
standard: It's Magic. Where
did it come from? From twenty-five
years in the same bed. It's Magic.

ROGER J. CROTTY

Walking in Monet's Gardens at Giverny

With my husband of eighteen years, down a path
of pink tulips in a drift of forget-me-nots.
The whole garden, in fullest bloom:
poppies, peonies, lupines, a rainbow of iris.
The willows bend their green veils
over the water lily pool. We stop on the footbridge,
framed in wisteria: waterfalls singing with bees.
How we forget to love one another,
in the tangle of everyday life.
Let us lie down and love, here in the flowers,
kiss my skin, for it is petals, the velvet falls of iris,
the heart of the peony, its voluptuous curves.
Let us become flowers, casual and gorgeous
in our brief hour, in this iris-scented air,
this light of cut glass and fine wine,
for already the petals are starting to fall,
they cover the ground in a dusting of snow.

BARBARA CROOKER

❧

LATER YEARS

Husband Song

I would be with you
in old age.
I would be tenderly wiping
the milk from your fierce gray beard,
holding your arm as we cross the street
slowly.

I would be with you
in old age,
saving you from sitting alone
like the men you saw through lit doorways
off the dark corridors of the houses where
you lived.

We will rock together on some porch
whose posts are twined with morning glory,
whistling bird calls into the night.

PENNY HARTER

I HELD HER HAND LIKE PORCELAIN

I held her hand like porcelain, delicate, round,
and felt the map of the world, a landscape told
by rivers blue that coursed a skin now browned
by the sun, made tough by pain, the crease and fold
of life. The hand that stroked the skin of baby,
the hand that stirred the soup, made the cakes
for all occasions, did the wash, folded the laundry,
the hand that held the rope of give and take,
became wondrous mirror in whose face I saw
the resplendence of a woman; and felt the love
  that flowed
from altar to this day—all told fifty years.
By her side, I watched hills full of glow
and traced the skin from sun to sun, to the window
where a blossom came to gently rest
on the miracle of tomorrow.

RAMNATH SUBRAMANIAN

Epithalamium

Although he is still surprised
That it has turned out this way
After all the years when
It seemed it wouldn't,

My father loves my mother
So much that there are times when
He is afraid he is going to die
Of it, the anxiety,

And there are times when
He thinks that would be a relief,
Better than the dis-ease of heart
That awaits him when she goes.

With his arthritic fingers
He threads the needle
She can no longer see
The eye of.

KELLY CHERRY

BOOK LOVERS

They come slowly into the library
with uneven steps;
she in a walker,
he on a cane,
one hand guiding her.

They scan the new books
and choose a few.
"Be sure it's something
you like, too," she says
as she hands him her choices.
He nods, knowing he'll be reading
some of the pages to her.

They turn to leave,
he tucking her scarf
around her head
against the anticipated wind.
He carries her books.

SHIRLEY NELSON

TRANSITION

The house is sold, the dooryard sign is down.
The buyer and the owner now agreed
This lovely home within a country town
Is perfect for a brand-new dweller's need.
We've packed our things and made the final move.
It's time to make adjustments, change our style.
In senior years we found the way to prove
Apartment life will bring a cheery smile.
No backward looks, we vowed, no tearful glance.
Transition is a part of growing old.
We'll put our thoughts on all that will advance
Security and comfort manifold.
Goodbye, old house, dear partner and good friend.
Our memories of you will never end!

JEAN CONDER SOULE

LONG RUN PLAY

Amateurs
we opened
without rehearsal
without repertoire
to mixed reviews
Learned
to revise the script
to play
with or without
supporting cast
Our dialogue costumes
have altered
The scenery shifts
time passes
our technique improves
We now use
a minimum of props
dispense
with makeup masks
and stand-ins
No longer vie for billing

MAUDE MEEHAN

IN THE COMFORT ZONE

Here in the comfort of years together
we sit on either side of the lamp.
Now and then one of us looks up
from our reading. One of us
speaks, and the other only
half hears but knows what is said
because all has already been said
and only the mellowness remains.

IDA FASEL

STILL LIFE

We have stretched past
our middle years, olive trees
ready for the late autumn pressing.

Our children are grown, ripe as Bosc pears.
Our grandchildren are in the vineyard
awaiting their first cutting.

Our fathers are asleep in the field.
Our mothers walk in the mist
toward the furrows.

Some of our leaves have faded;
some pile up on dried grasses.
But we still have patches

of cobalt green and yellow ochre
layered on us with a kind palette knife.
The light still comes from the east.

We gently await
the artist's next brush stroke;
savoring this stolen season.

DONNA WAHLERT

&

IN SICKNESS

Living Will

At fifty, I prepare for widowhood
after my husband's second heart attack.

We dispense instructions:
This is where I keep bank records,
here's how to download photos
from the digital camera to the computer.

His garden is the last domain to surrender.
I follow my husband out back when he asks
Do you want to see how I gather lettuce?

He shows me how to peel layers from plants
before the sun becomes overbearing.
We harvest what remains after insects
nibble crochetlike holes in the greens.

Each leaf trembles in our hands
like a Tibetan prayer flag,
beseeching.

MARY KOLADA SCOTT

FOR BETTER, FOR WORSE

Worse arrived so soon—Cancer.
Twenty-eight, we'd barely begun:
Two young children, our first house.

We hoped against hope
it wasn't as bad as it sounded.
But worse had come to stay,

entwining itself into our lives—
surgery, radiation, chemotherapy,
dizzying cycles of expectation and loss,

painfully rescued time, five years
fending off truth. But all the while,
unbeknownst to us, better had slipped

through our door as well. Little things,
disappointments with each other, petty
annoyances, began to disappear.

Our best selves, the ones we'd pledged
on our wedding day, discovered
nothing is better than together.

MARYANNE O'BRYAN

IF WE LET IT

Grandma fell down
Down the basement steps
Whether the stroke came before
Or after
Does not matter
She was never there again
In the way that she had been

What matters is the way that Grandpa
Cared for her each day
Without complaint
Treated her with tenderness
And somehow found still within
The one he had loved and lived with
As he bathed
        calmed
              fed her
And how five years after her fall when she
Died (after their sixty-eighth anniversary) he mourned

*In
Sickness*
❀ 124 ❀

What matters is what we saw, we

Twenty-six grandchildren

That love can grow ever so

Deep

    Strong

        True

If we are willing

If we let it

JIM CROEGAERT

For My Wife in the Bone Marrow Unit

Ah, Dame, I don't know how else to love you
sometimes, so I just start juggling. I'm on the street

three floors below your hospital window,
lofting fish or birds that graze against my hands

and fly off; juggling cancer cells and carnations,
slipping in the bowling pin I

snuck out of the alley in Maine. Then I'm juggling
freight trains, and angels, and elephants,

dropping them all. I don't care. So long
as you can stand near your high window and laugh,

so long as you stand near your hospital bed
clapping your hands.

JOHN RYBICKI

LOVE . . . AND CHEMO

In the midst of our greatest challenge
I am reminded of what brought us together—
When the eyes of the hand I am holding
Tell me
"You'll still be beautiful when you're bald."

MARY MAUDE DANIELS

TOUCH

In the recovery room, with the plastic cap
still on my head, I say,
"It hurts. Rub something."

My husband appears the next morning
to spend nine hours
working his fingers into my shoulders, back,
arms, legs, thighs, hips, face.

With his touch, I feel my body
slowly ease away from distress.
A buoyancy returns,
an awareness of life.

My partner of over fifty years
carefully turns me on my side.
I close my eyes
and muse:
tomorrow will be
a better day.

BLANCHE ROSLOFF

After His Second Heart Attack: A Psalm

How many miracles can I ask for, O Lord?
How many times can I come to your door?
I have paced before your entryway so many times
that the carpet is threadbare.
You have always answered my knock
and given me the bread that I needed.
I have thanked you, but not enough.
My knees should be tattered as the carpet.
Yet, here I am again, persistent
like the woman with a hemorrhage
stubbornly asking to touch the hem of your garment.
All I want is to feel that linen woven with light
and implore you to heal my husband
and ask you to give me peace.
My heart feels so threadbare.

DONNA WAHLERT

PORCELAIN FRAGMENTS

My plate is overflowing:
a breast half dead
your injured heart
my wounded arm
your damaged toes.
Today I will garnish us
with mangos and marionberries
sip the juice
that drips so sweet
from the heat of us.
Haltingly
you touch my tarnished breast
tenderly
I trace the ridges of your chest scar.
Under down as soft as sweet dreams
our legs entwine;
yours so long and strong
mine so wide and soft.

Tonight
we soak ourselves in lips of wine
holding the fragile porcelain fragments
of ourselves together
for one more time.

ROSALIND LEVINE

MY HUSBAND'S FIRST TIME OUT
SINCE THE DIAGNOSIS

We set up folding chairs along the curb
to watch the Mill Valley Fourth of July Parade:

The color-blind town librarian in pink stiletto heels,
red sequined overalls, and orange baseball cap,

Boy Scouts, their chests bulging with more
badges than I could count,

Waving local officials, having
requisitioned every convertible in the valley,

A gaggle of golden retrievers in red bandannas,
tongues hanging out like water slides,

A bicycle brigade, featuring
the whole town's population under puberty,

The volunteer Dad's Marching Band,
loud and enthusiastic if not quite in sync,

The finale, a fire truck, one slightly peeved
Dachshund in a miniature helmet, seated aloft.

Fire fighters hurled hard candies. Everyone
rushed out and fought to scoop them up,

as if they were semiprecious stones,
Tahitian pearls or winning lottery tickets.

Then when the parade had passed, when the thirsty
howlings of dogs had ceased, when the last trail of

engine smoke had cleared and, pockets bulging
with goodies, children began to stagger off,

My husband turned to me and slowly spoke his first
words in two weeks, "Needs more elephants!"

SUSAN R. NORTON

HELPLESS

Words too painful to
comprehend were captured
by your ears. The eyes
reacted, withholding
tears yet expressing
terror. Metastatic
carcinoma, advanced.
I held your hand but
could not hold back your
dying.

LOIS GREENE STONE

THIRTEEN

PARTINGS

THIS LOVE

This love.
This space.
This minuscule of time we share
is sheltered in our hearts.

These precious fleeting moments,
cherished with tender understanding,
nurtured by endless encouragement,
sustained by unbelievable strength,
find chambers in which to rest.

When the clock strikes
and the chimes of time slow
or ring no more,
each shining moment will rise
and fill the quiet space
with joy and laughter,
and music

and we will dance our finest dance,
and touch,
and feel,
and love, my dear,
once more.

MARY LENORE QUIGLEY

AFTEREFFECTS

It's the next day and you do not appear. For the longest time, I pray you will emerge, like fruit from a fertile blossom. Pain and fear begin to erode my happiness because I have seen the fate of an ember outside the flame. Every inch of my stomach hurts. My head aches as I wonder how a paper kite with stocking tails, lifted to the sky and released on an unknown course, fares. I am a heavy stone in deep water.

JOHARI AKILI

ALONE

Alone,
I pull the heating pad
under the small of my back,
listen to its little buzzing sounds,
finger the braille spots
that tell me how warm.
I fall asleep.
Waking too hot,
I press my palms to the cold
window glass above my head,
throw the heating pad under the bed.
I miss you.

PENNY HARTER

THE WIDOW

I sharpen these knives
at the angle you taught me
sliding stone against steel,
recalling your hands around mine
by the kitchen sink, long ago.

Now, I take out the garbage cans,
fill the birdfeeder, mow grass
and monthly pay the bills;
I sign my name
in the lower right-hand corner
as though that name
had always been my own;
but it is your name

as the tackle box and rods are yours,
and the waders which still lean
against the hall closet's inside wall.
Yours, this fountain pen,
these regimented ledger books,
subscription to a magazine
I never read. In your name,

which you shared with me
until I thought of it as ours.

And nothing, now, is ours—
or yours, as I once was.
Whether you assigned it
with ownership or tenderness,
you can no longer reclaim
anything which bears your name.

Nor will you ever again sharpen
the edge of this paring knife,
or put your hands
around my hands, here,
by the kitchen sink.

ANN E. MICHAEL

DRIVING ALONE

I ride roller coasters now.
You'd be shocked, even resentful
to see me with the kids
swaying swiftly side to side
lurching forward in the darkness.
I'm not afraid anymore.
No ride could be as rough
as the black limousine
coming home from your funeral.
I've survived what I didn't care to survive,
and now, with grim determination
I test new strengths.
The wife who used to stay home
for a snowflake
now drives to work on icy roads.
I check tires, arrange repairs,
read maps, navigate at night.
All the qualms you used to cajole
have collided
into the single challenge
of driving alone.

JACQUELINE JULES

At the Cimitiére de Montmartre

We came down the hill from Montmartre,
disappointed that it was full of Americans
from the Place du Têtre to Sacré Coeur,
and ended up at the lacy iron gates
of the cemetery, laid out like a small city,
long shady avenues, houses of marble and stone,
sunlight filtered through acacia trees.

We looked for the graves of the famous:
Berlioz, Truffaut, Émile Zola,
resting near the merely ordinary
in the dance of shadows and light. We sat
on a wrought iron bench, ate camembert,
pain de compagne, a kilo of cherries,
and for a sweet moment, I loved you so completely,
when I die, I want our ashes to mingle, bury us in
   earth,
plant a rose bush, let it grow thorny, tangled,
and covered in blossoms; I want there to be no
separation between my skin and yours.

BARBARA CROOKER

Passage

If I should be the first to go
Mourn not the grave I lie,
Although the chair is empty
My spirit did not die.

Death is not a foe to fear
When mortal time is through.
The tears I shed are sadness
At thoughts of leaving you.

I'll miss your cherished love,
The look, the touch that said
When one of us was hurt—
The other always bled.

Memories are the blessing
That endures beyond the dust;
We accept the will of God
And do the things we must.

If I should be the first to go
I'll mark the path with care
So when you follow in my steps—
You'll find me waiting there.

C. DAVID HAY

ON VALENTINE'S DAY

An old man got on a bus one February 14th, carrying a dozen roses. He sat behind a young man. The young man looked at the roses and said, "Somebody's going to get a beautiful Valentine's Day gift."

"Yes," said the old man.

A few minutes went by and the old man noticed that his young companion was staring at the roses. "Do you have a girlfriend?" the old man asked.

"I do," said the young man. "I'm going to see her right now, and I'm going to give her this Valentine's Day card."

They rode in silence for another ten minutes, and then the old man got up to get off the bus. As he stepped out into the aisle, he suddenly placed the roses on the young man's lap and said, "I think my wife would want you to have these. I'll tell her I gave them to you."

He left the bus quickly. As the bus pulled away, the young man turned to see the old man enter the gates of a cemetery.

AUTHOR UNKNOWN

SEASONS LOST

The Seasons came and passed again
Since last I heard your voice;
Many are the ways I'd change
If death but gave a choice.

I'd pick you flowers in the Spring
To show you that I care
And when you need comforting
You'd always find me there.

The Summer breeze against my cheek
Like memories of your touch;
The love we take for granted
Is the one we miss so much.

Sunlight on the Autumn leaves,
Reflections of your hair;
Youth and beauty paid the price—
God often takes the fair.

Winter winds that chill the heart
And etch your stone with frost,
Whisper of eternal love
Beyond the years we lost.

C. DAVID HAY

ALONE IS AN EMPTY HOUSE

Alone is an empty house,
each room echoing memories,
years of smiles, days of love.
Your spirit is still with me, though.
Sometimes I think I hear your steps.
I feel your hand in mine.
Heaven has blessed me with these dreams.
Alone, I know you'll always be
alive in my heart.

MARION SCHOEBERLEIN

MUSIC, WHEN SOFT VOICES DIE

Music, when soft voices die,
Vibrates in the memory—
Odours, when sweet violets sicken,
Live within the sense they quicken.

Rose leaves, when the rose is dead,
Are heap'd for the beloved's bed;
And so thy thoughts, when thou art gone,
Love itself shall slumber on.

PERCY BYSSHE SHELLEY
(1792–1822)

Partings
❧ 151 ❧

YOU ARE STILL HERE

Remembrance brings me face to face.
The wish to see makes seeing
The place where light outshines the dark—
The very depths of being.

Time took you from me and restores.
Long as I live, you do.
The night stars glisten for us both.
Morning glories open blue

Each day, for each day yields the truth:
The heart alone outweighs
The pain and carries us beyond
The count of absent days.

Our words without words form and move—
Move presence into mind.
There is no power that can part
Lives so intertwined.

IDA FASEL

Be with Me

Be with me through the quiet end—
From the here and now.

With your familiar breath,
Whisper closely, softly, sweetly,
Words of comfort and love.

Set my heart to heaven's door,
Help me turn the key.
For now I'll love you more than life,
For all eternity.

ANNIE DOUGHERTY

MIGRATION

after *Invention with Migratory Birds* by José Bedia

We have always known
we would leave with a flight
of migrating birds, our naked
bodies rising from the earth,
our cooling flesh framed
in starlight.

We have been stumbling for years
toward this departure—
their wings like blades
rowing the dark, their beaks
lifting us on luminous cords

toward the place where winter
is a blessing, and they
are the sun.

PENNY HARTER

REFLECTIONS

MARRIAGE

At first vows,
marriage needs to be nurtured
like a newborn babe.
Swaddle it in trust
powder it with common goals
nourish it with affirmations to
make it grow healthy and unique.

As it gets older and rock solid,
entertain it with laughter
feed it with conversation
pepper it with honesty
salt it with acceptance.

Later in life
as it eases into middle years,
caress it with understanding
praise its uniqueness
celebrate its ripening age,
a union grown strong
through time and tears.

SUSAN R. NORTON

Loving the Distance Between Them

Once the realization is accepted that even between the closest human beings infinite distances continue to exist, a wonderful living side by side can grow up, if they succeed in loving the distance between them which makes it possible for each to see the other whole against the sky.

RAINER MARIA RILKE
(1875-1926)

What Counts

What counts in making a happy marriage is not
so much how compatible you are, but how you deal
with imcompatibility.

LEO TOLSTOY
(1828–1910)

Once in a Lifetime

After all these years together,
my mind can't help but wonder
if it's even possible to re-create
with others a love we've managed
to build together, day by day,
word by word, deed by deed.

Perhaps the gods, jealous
of mere mortals such as we,
allow only one almost perfect
communion of hearts and souls
in a single lifetime.

SUSAN R. NORTON

THE LIVING DREAM

Maybe love is just not taking for granted
simple pleasures that are complex to others
who don't enjoy popcorn after potpies,
a walk around the block
with a willful Yorkshire terrier or
reruns of *7th Heaven*
in winter or summer,
two or more curled up on one sofa
after baths have bubbled
and we're falling asleep
almost at the same time, more or less.

I used to think love had to be
Fourth of July, but now I wonder
as all desires change in time
into true concern if eternal bliss
just seems to endure
longer like sound of waves
and the taste of any kiss
making the present into
tomorrow's memories.

ROCHELLE LYNN HOLT

THE GREATEST BLESSING IN MARRIAGE

Perhaps the greatest blessing in marriage is that it lasts so long, The years, like the varying interests of each year, combine to buttress and enrich each other. Out of many shared years, one life. In a series of temporary relationships, one misses the ripening, gathering, harvesting joys, the deep, hard-won truths of marriage.

RICHARD C. CABOT
(1855–1916)

Marriage Is a Spiritual Contract

Marriage is a spiritual contract,
a dovetail joint of two souls
beyond religious beliefs or
cultural design. It sets hearts
into a framework where
what you put in is what you receive.

It's a cosmic abode where the balance
of sun and moon dwells: strong
through the winds of change,
bright as Venus
on a clear night when joy
makes its home in your joining.

Marriage is you and me
as we celebrate the fire,
day in and day out,
our very breath
the bellows of
Love.

ARLENE GAY LEVINE

Author Index

PERMISSIONS AND ACKNOWLEDGMENTS

Grateful acknowledgment is made to the authors and publishers for the use of the following material. Every effort has been made to contact original sources. If notified, the publishers will be pleased to rectify an omission in future editions.

Johari Akili for "Aftereffects."

Coleman Barks for "My First Love Story" and
  "This Night."

Virginia Barrett for "Request."

Ellen Bass for "Basket of Figs" and "Sleeping with You"
  from *Mules of Love*, copyright © 2002 by Ellen Bass.
  Reprinted with permission of BOA Editions, Ltd.

Ann Reisfeld Boutté for "Warranty."

Janine Canan for "My Heart," "Night Secret," and
  "A Love Song."

Kirsten Casey for "Last Name."

Moushumi Chakrabarty for "Say."

Kelly Cherry for "Appoggiatura" and "Epithalamium."

Jennifer Lynn Clay for "Him."

Elayne Clift for "Marriage Work."

Deborah Gordon Cooper for "In This Season."

Jim Croegaert for "If We Let It."

Barbara Crooker for "At the Cimitiére de Montmartre," "Away in Virginia, I See a Mustard Field and Think of You," "In the Middle," "Tenth Anniversary," "Ordinary Life," "Possibly," and "Walking in Monet's Gardens at Giverny."

Roger J. Crotty for "Magic."

Mary Maude Daniels for "Love . . . and Chemo."

Annie Dougherty for "Be with Me."

Lori Eberhardy for "Beloved," "A Heart Full of Love," and "The Kiss."

Ida Fasel for "Choices," "First House," "You Are Still Here," and "In the Comfort Zone."

Maureen Tolman Flannery for "Their Adventures," "Long After the Loss," and "Summer on the Farm."

Charles Ghigna for "Give Me Ten More Years," "From the Astronaut of Your Heart," and "The Blues."

Ingrid Goff-Maidoff for "Questions," "At the Half-Chance of Being Loved," and "To Turn from My Forgetting."

Arlene Gay Levine for "The Gift," "Unconditional,"
  and "Marriage I s a Spiritual Contract."
Rosalind Levine for "Porcelain Fragments."
Nancy Tupper Ling for "Another New England Winter."
Stephen J. Lyons for "Gratitude" and "Remembering."
Maude Meehan for "Long Run Play."
Ann E. Michael for "The Widow."
Dawn B. Mundy for "For My Beloved."
Shirley Nelson for "Book Lovers."
Joan Noëldechen for "In Transit."
Susan R. Norton for "Once in a Lifetime," "My
  Husband's First Time Out Since the Diagnosis,"
  "Marriage," "After All These Years of Loving You,"
  and "Small Failures as a Wife."
Marian Olson for "In the Light of Another Moon."
Nita Penfold for "Why."
Andrea Potos for "Roots."
Mary Lenore Quigley for "This Love."
Zoraida Rivera Morales for "Love Life."
Jean Roach for "Transforming Love."
Marjorie Rommel for "Seeing You."

Blanche Rosloff for "Touch."

Jo-Anne Rowley for "Love Poem."

John Rybicki for "For My Wife in the Bone
Marrow Unit."

Barbara Schmitz for "Husband Out of Town Thinks
About His Wife."

Marion Schoeberlein for "Alone Is an Empty House."

Mary Kolada Scott for "Double Image" and "Living
Will." "Double Image" was originally published
in *Proposing on the Brooklyn Bridge: Poems
about Marriage* (Grayson Books, 2003).

Pearl Stein Selinsky for "Finding Us in Jackson
Pollack," which was previously published in
Golden Words and *Hodgepodge*.

Leah Kathryn Sell for "You, I Hope to Find."

Sherri Waas Shunfenthal for "First Kiss."

Bob Slaymaker for "My Wife Breaks Out."

Jean Conder Soule for "Transition."

Cassie Premo Steele for "How to Return to Your
Husband."

Lois Greene Stone for "Helpless."

Ramnath Subramanian for "I Held Her Hand Like
Porcelain."

Donna Wahlert for "After His Second Heart Attack:
A Psalm," "Upon Awakening," "Anniversary," and
"Still Life."

About the Author

June Cotner is an accomplished author, anthologist, and speaker. Her books altogether have sold more than 750,000 copies. June has appeared on national radio programs and her books have been featured in many national publications, including *USA Today, Better Homes & Gardens, Woman's Day*, and *Family Circle*. She teaches workshops and gives presentations at bookstores throughout the country and at the Pacific Northwest Writer's Association Conference, the Pacific Northwest Booksellers Association Conference, and the Learning Annex centers in New York and California. With her consulting business, June shares her knowledge of writing strong and successful proposals.

A graduate of the University of California at Berkeley, June is the mother of two grown children and lives in Poulsbo, Washington, with her husband, two dogs, and one cat. Her hobbies include yoga, hiking, clogging, and cross-country skiing.

For more information, visit June's Web site at www.junecotner.com.